Behind Her City Eyes

poems by

Sarah Erin

New York, New York

Cover Work by Hollis Jo McCollum

Visit our website:
www.21chieftanspress.com

THIRD EDITION
ISBN: 979-8-218-17061-5
Produced in the United States of America

Nicole

You are my Cristina Yang.
Thank you for guiding me through
every emotion about the woman who
inspired this poetry collection.

"I love you a thousand yellow daisies."

"I find it hard to believe you don't know the beauty that you are, but if you don't, let me be your eyes."

The Velvet Underground

Behind Her City Eyes

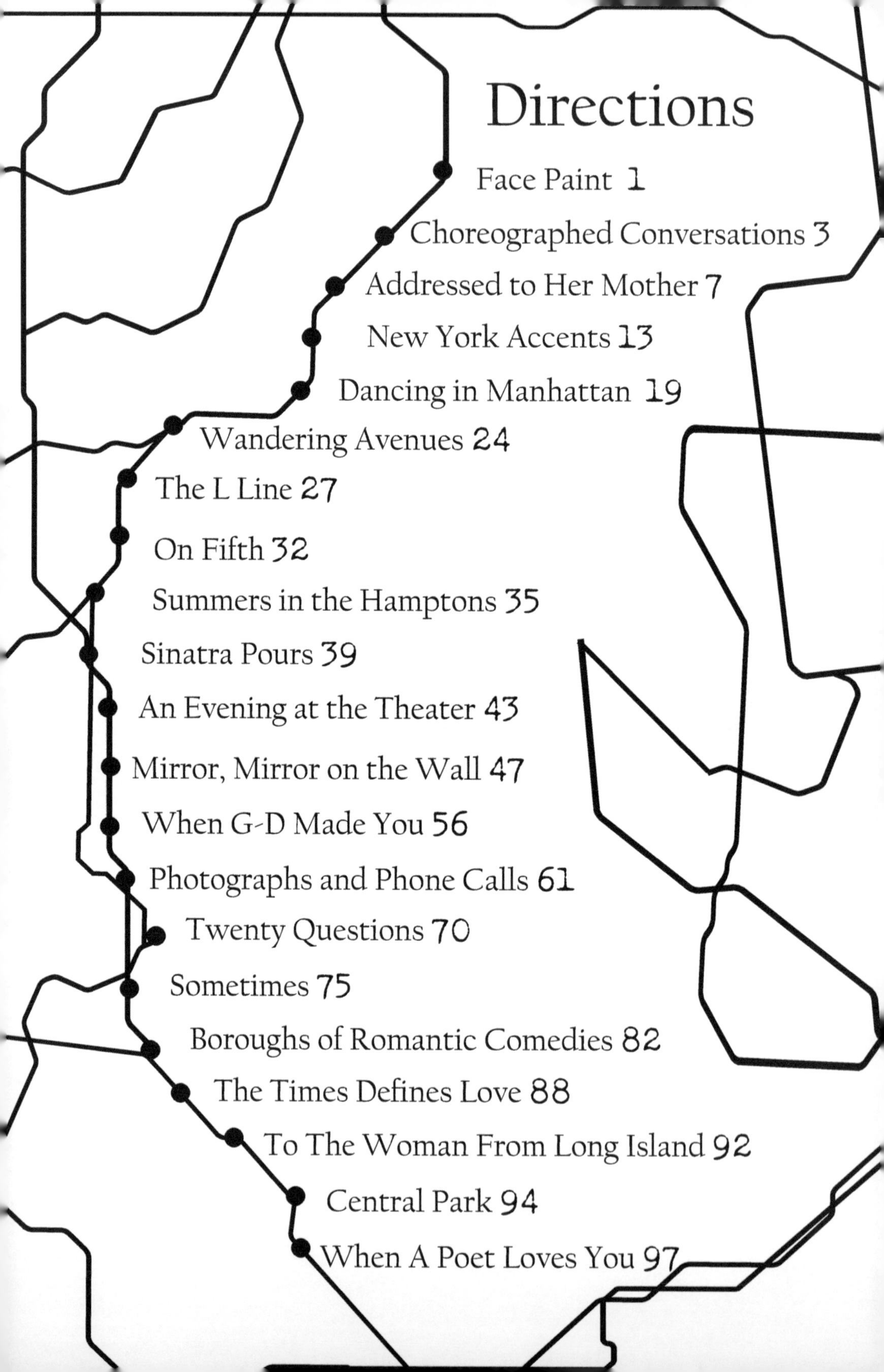

Directions

FACE PAINT

Each morning, when you put on your makeup,
are you as elated as your reflection shows
or is that when anxiety conceals your appearance?

a masking foundation:
  rouged rosy cheeks, primed lips
  tinted with a shell shaded gloss
    to hide a lost, naked fear
    a shaky brush
    dusting the pigment of uncertainty
    your eyelids shadowed with a crippling,
                cracked sixth sense:
                worry—
              your smudged mascara
              is unable to run from
you dropped the pallet
yet you still manage to apply it perfectly
as if it never slipped at all

    I speculate

    why that need for control
    unknowingly controls you.

        Although
from what I can remember about this routine
I imagine, it must be quite captivating,
    capturing your art—

    the minuscule changes you've made,
    to watch you prepare for the day.

Each time the brush sweeps across your face
or the liner frames your eyes

what do you see?

what do you think about
while setting your face with powder,
and inspecting the subtly blushed canvas?

Because what I see is a stunning work of art,
and I’m afraid that you only see the paint.

CHOREOGRAPHED CONVERSATIONS

It feels like I have known you
for my entire life…
and yet—

I know nothing about you at all.

You
are the seven years of ballet training
        I wished to excel at as a little girl
        practicing arduously to measure up
        buying every tap shoe and leotard
                        praising the craft

        feeling boundless pleasure— twirling endlessly
        a sense of belonging, confidently
          embraced
                          by the stage

        yet unable to perfect the choreography
        f a l l i n g
        out of the routine,
        now wishing I could reposition my feet
        but the steps require one plié too many
          now terribly strenuous on my knees

              I gleefully immerse myself
              in the nostalgia of the spotlight
              the familiarity of their warmth

          absorbed
        into the core of my being
              just as you are

It's difficult for me to picture
the details of your green room
how you prefer your tea
what you rush to put on the tv…

I hanker for deep, unique moments with you.
painting gel acrylic portraits
with the polish of my memories

nails tapping on the glass as your mother would
filling gaps of speech or thinking silently
tabling her thoughts for later

so remembering
who you are
is just a fresh OPI
Ballet Slipper
french manicure away.

I pray for sincere conversations between us.

but

We have never consistently stayed in touch
developed much—

so why do I feel

c l o s e r?

My most vulnerable desire, is for you to care
about me enough
to pick up the phone

unprompted

and actually discuss our lives…
not surface level asides

like my college major
the inclement weather
or whether I'm dating

someone

single
me
out

learn something authentic about me
give me
a truthful glimpse
of you

covering eleven years' time
picking up as quickly as
the tick of metronome I'd outgrow

when stage fright

in competition with my devotion

achieved the lead

spinning ahead of my intention to keep dancing
leaving our meaningful relationship

behind

Although
I crave knowing each other so well

that my sense of humor oscillates with yours
a sarcastic classic ballet

synched to a melody of clacking platforms
turnouts stretching giggles, pirouettes of unraveling laughter
pointe shoes laced with inside jokes — we count combos
lead by the tightly knotted bow
the present of your dependable arms

I yearn for the day when I can sit across from you
and know the delicate choreography

swaying to the rhythm
of your inner monologue

by looking into your eyes
reading the music they hide

intuitively knowing what to sing

ADDRESSED TO HER MOTHER

It pains me to know that you might not approve

of me

loving your daughter.

not because we are both women
I know you'd be supportive of me in that sense—
but because of what our names signify

the severity of Capulet and Montague
Shakespeare couldn't manage the ripple effect
a romantic relationship between us would do

considering this instance is far from possible
listed in the dictionary defining ridiculous, unrealistic,

out of the question

questioning the applicable examples
under the italics
like

what could I provide for her?

when
that's not even a factor.

or what would revealing
this accomplish?

when that level of vulnerability
causes a *claustrophobia*

an intensified panic to leave
when the ability to identify
uncharted emotions *crushes*
us
confined
in disquieting territory.

I would like to believe that we could chat
over coffee, let me pose what's troubling
my instincts — maybe exchange stories…

You could tell me
what she was like
when she was young
and I could thank you
for bringing her into my life…

How do you think she turned out?
Does she seem *fulfilled* to you?
Joyful even?

She rarely opens up to anyone,
let alone to me
it's difficult to find
what makes her chime

a grandfather clock passed midnight
secondhand calls from the opposite hall
a runway
running away from herself—
everyone else

while still wondering what time it is

So, I'm coming to you; the closest link I have
to the slinky of questions

s

p

i

r

a

l

i

n

g

down the stairs
staring directly into mystery's eyes

What role did you play in that?

I'm sorry— It's just
I've heard a multitude of things,

it's hard to know
what to believe
anymore

Why is there a shield of armor
worn by a steadfast, unrelenting knight
diligently guarding any mention of you?

What battles has she fought
that the thought of you
repels her from disrobing the metal cage
keeping you at the sharper end of swords distance

I feel so conflicted.

Every bone in my body, has shifted alignment
focused on breaking,
eradicating the joints
of my cracking emotions.

Now that I have voiced them to someone,
I feel as though I can't deny them
any
longer
my once protected skeleton has snapped
with every letter
in each word

which travels the aching structure
my arthritic anatomy
from mouth, to ears,

from hand to pen,
and back again

posted for continuous delivery—
The seal on my envelope has torn,
tattered
been tampered with

I am incapable of managing the mail

becoming the postwoman
you never gave your address to
who
travels her route
wondering where to forward herself

this letter will never be read

since death

doesn't have a mailbox.

The perplexing part isn't identifying the grief
anchored to the ship of lost time with you

or my obviously undeniable
affection toward your daughter

it is that
for some bizarre reason,
I still feel
you are a sail in the wind
steering my thoughts
peering over my shoulder
as I write

acknowledging how
I've continued to respect

Your tenacity
your boldness,
your attitudes about romance, passion,
sex
relationships in general —

aside from mine with her.

you exuded a feisty fearlessness
when it came to pushing against
the expected path
laid tile by tile

a cemented position

most casted you out for
but you scraped it up and set down your own

I have always wished to emulate

s e p a r a t i n g
from the patterns

I indubitably
g r e w
into

sewing patches of my own
gathered in a fabric cabinet

fraying at the edges of my mind

But my love for your daughter
makes sorting through these prints
exceedingly complicated

Even though
there is a slight chance of you
at least attempting to understand my feelings

you have been absent in her mind
for a considerable amount of time

and I can't think about her
without thinking of you
too.

NEW YORK ACCENTS

New York accents
have a strange calming quality to them.

Maybe
it's because I grew up around them,
and basically

e v e r y o n e

I hold dear
seems to have one,

especially
you

Any time I am anxious
or otherwise distraught

hearing your voice
and its distinctive qualities,
is the ultimate cure for my homesickness

my intense longing for a city stroll
for the sleeplessness
gnawing at my drowsy
dreamer's soul

you are the blissful beacon—
the lighthouse which marks
my essence complete,
the harbor which makes it whole

When I am near you,
I can pick out your voice
from anyone else's in the room.

I don't know why,
but your accent
has

a l w a y s

sounded unique to me.

Maybe
it's the pitch of your voice
in combination with the accent,
or maybe
it's the fact that
when I hear your voice,
it unleashes a

f l u t t e r i n g
family of butterflies

wings spanning from cheek to cheek
emerging from a chrysalis
affectionately blooming dozens of roses
inside the vase of my dimples

vibrant hues,
stemming from cute disarray
when you say my name

Overarching joy consumes my brain

gliding through my body— drifting in the atmosphere
as I whimsically fly around the gravity

of your presence

the monarch
with a sensitive tan
iridescently pink aura

bridging the gap
between overthinking and relief

an aura
that grows gardens
gifted with the seeds
of feeling seen

they sprout from the ground in an instant
and live far past the expectancy
of the oldest oaks

I can't pinpoint when I was originally able
to distinguish your accent from every other
New Yorker around us when you spoke

but I do remember the
p r e c i s e
moment

I realized

I was in love with you.

You stepped foot into the restaurant
parting the sea of gloomy weather

surfing the wave between
will it rain or will it snow

from the party going on inside
tables lined with appetizers

people eating, seated with each other, speaking
pools of New York accents playing racquetball
bouncing off the walls

it all came to an abrupt halt for me
forming a tunnel— vision of absolute beauty

dressed to the nines in midnight undertones
mingling with dusk, thoughtful anecdotes
made by metallic stars

leaving such an impression on me
I fossilized— a state of weightlessness
formed a cloud mesmerized by the sky

your meteor hits
r a d i a t i n g

brightly like the newly lit
Christmas Tree in Rockefeller Center.

It was electrifying
how
with the flip of a switch
all the years I've known you

suddenly shown each memory—
conducting individual bulbs

they glowed
like garland adorned with ornaments
signifying every season I've spent with you

I had never truly seen
the power of your magnificence,
until that day.

I specifically recall pining over
how vibrant your laugh sounded

recognizing the scent
of that pine tree in the air

reminding me
of the cheerfulness

in the heartfelt nature
of your nurturing smile.

I go back to that day in my mind quite often
missing you

listening to
how a silver bell merrily rings
astutely attune to how astonishing you are

hearing the December in your voice
invariably brings me back
to your melodically, unmistakable
New York accent

that seems to alleviate

and kick-start

my aggressively beating heart

somehow

s y n c h r o n o u s l y

DANCING IN MANHATTAN

I can see the reflection of the record player
    spinning from the bedroom window

        while I sit in bed rain and frost form
                    tiny glaciers, icicles

  dangling along the perimeter
  of the daintily decorated slightly
                  open frame

The curtains are blowing in the subtle wind
      early morning breaths
      winter sighs of the city.

I can't quite place
the expression on your face

observing your reflection
leaves you slightly blurred

I turn
to watch you stare into the dawning sunrise
you resemble a scene straight out of a film…

The effortless waves
shaping the ends of your blonde curls
      captivate my gaze.

resting just below your shoulders
an intricate snowflake impeccably placed
                  as if right on the nose.

The beautiful outlines of your body
practically painted by Picasso

are snuggled tightly in the top sheet
you clung to when you left me in bed,
calming the brisk,
yet cozy
cold

through the small opening the city permits
for windows above the fifth floor

as you twist away from it,
fixating your attention on me

I become the only person in existence

apart
from you

The minute we lock eyes, I slowly rise
take baby steps from the bed
heading in your direction.

You inch backwards
now up against the rapidly
freezing window

while I continue forward
until my hand leaves an impression on the glass
pinning you as I caress your jaw with my thumb
then kiss you.

In awe of your elegance,
I draw you into my embrace
and guide us to the center of the room.

Tangled in top sheet, we gently sway
as Unchained Melody begins to play.

Our lovable laughter floods the apartment
as we move in tandem—

back
and
forth

in a spontaneous steady rhythm

Tripping over ourselves repeatedly,
certainly separates us from partners
on *Dancing With The Stars*

Nevertheless,
the twinkle in your eye
makes my heart trill

sends chills along my spine

you are a breath of the freshest air
New York City lungs have
ever known

I exhale,
and a slight shudder escapes my mouth;
you use your finger to trace my lips.

You
Are

I n t o x i c a t i n g

your heat is steamier than a fresh cup of cocoa

crafted with luxurious
Fifth Dimension chocolate
as decadent as your eyes

Pushing your bangs off your face,
I glide my hand stroking your cheek
smooth
like the sweetness of you
pouring peppermint from each pore

wide-eyed sliding my palm along your neck
down your throat... to your chest...

your breath
gets
considerably deeper
I can see—
g
o
o
s
e
b
u
m
p
s
as the top sheet is peeled
from beneath your hair
your shoulders then
s
l
i
p
s
to the floor.

Before I can direct the pads of my fingers
to your torso, you feverishly grab my wrist
and
p u l l
me back into bed

I kiss your lips with every ounce
of passion, I can possibly muster.

you whisper
p l e a s e
make love to me

I trail my way
b
e
l
o
w
your waist

ready to taste that
long awaited
sugar

I hear the record player begin to

c r a c k l e

the needle lifts

I open my eyes
and
you're gone

WANDERING AVENUES

A train chugs our love
on the railroad toward your home
I pass where you stop.

How tall must you rise?
eyes climb each fire escape
your sight is the ground.

Grasp art in those hands
your palms are the exhibit
lines, the gallery

Silhouettes, shadows
city streets glisten the rays
sunshine casts off you

While you lie awake
your essence fuels the morning
a gorgeous new day

Your curling iron
clamps beautifully blonde strands which
twirl and flip me too

Melt anxiety
like a strip of Listerine
your speech cleanses me

Swipe a metrocard
turnstiles grant me entry
which line follows you?

Security tight
who knows if you are alright
I am a tourist

Pretty lights, towers
make fantasies of concrete
you surpass them all

Traffic jams inch worm
tunnels direct millions home
all maps lead to you

Run late, never wait
jaywalking is efficient
as you cross my heart

Dinner and a show
people flock to the theater
to meet you, stage door

Though conscious or not
your irreplaceable part
casts a spotlight lost.

Purses, patterned scarves
undeniable class, charm
fashion suits you well

You hold yourself high
higher than the One World Trade
do you still fear flight

You turn keys, memories
nostalgic Natural History
please make more with me

Public Library
tales that hook readers, how you
pull love, from the shelves

Cobblestones, cool breeze
cups of tea, leaves, and the trees
paths your compass leads

Fall as in autumn
or falling in love with you
when will the leaves change?

Your face shimmers gold,
an untradable kindness
Wall Street yearns to gain

Aspirations gleam
my Statue of Liberty
you believed in me.

Ellis Island gate
opportunities galore
you granted freedom

Saturday market
freshest berries, bananas
coffee's not a meal

Your fruitful pollen
sweet, sheds tears painfully
wilting makes honey

Greenwich Ave cafés
write, coffee, breakfast all day
sights which capture you

Almond taste pastry
delectable like your eyes
brown cannot define.

THE L LINE

Why does the whoosh of the subway
rushing past me on the platform
feel identically comforting
to the sensation of your arms around me?

Your hugs
alert the megaphone of my mind
to stand carefully behind the yellow line
so I don't get swept away until the car
across the raised platform bumps
comes to an abrupt halt
triggers the latch on the automatic doors
and
I can
unfailingly step inside

anxiety flies
stranded on that platform
bombarded by mixed signals
unable to make out
the called names of each station

due to the inconveniently low volume
of the subway announcer coupled with
the ridiculously high volume
of the subway cars rattling
the wobbling
between each linked car
and the distracting sound
that the cars make as they speed along
the high voltage track

a knee-jerk reaction

falling for you shocked me
as obscured words mingling
with confused security
shakes me

into reliably reaching
my designated destination

these hallmarks of navigating the city
envelop me as I drift in the tunnel
of artificial wind
a love

that cools
no
calms
no
crashes me

faced with a balanced but bumpy reality

that I tried to stand clear of those doors
for an obscene amount of years

walking pavement lined with fear
feet bleeding muscles screaming along

as if outrunning the subway was feasible
as if sprinting would suddenly become more efficient
as if ignoring the somehow settling screeches
would prevent me
from honestly

admitting
I was kidding myself

by avoiding a soothing system
I could no longer make sense of

afraid of aimlessly pacing through
those underground tunnels of loving you

with the uneasy realization

I had no destination
lost in transportation

reading every station
sign
yet finding
immeasurable feet
tracking distance

riotously relieving
when hearing the announcer
tediously repeating

"Stand clear
of the closing doors, please."

doors
that
I kept
rushing
back
through
to a time
before I fully knew

why
they reminded me
of you

they still do.

the woman
who
focused my sight
traveled to my soul
then
blew
me
away

blew
me
away

so completely

I landed
stranded

somewhere on the Upper East
or is that
the other side
of me?

You became the primary direction
each line would eventually reach
streamlining my finding the way
to my self-aware
midtown mind

I smile

reminiscent of your guidance
every time that breeze
sweeps over me
you
have gotten me
exactly
where I needed to be

without
ever
letting
me
go

even when I intentionally refrained

from

taking
the
train

ON FIFTH

All department stores
with a designated perfume floor
seem to have their own signature scent
despite carrying an extensive number of sets
made by every brand you could possibly imagine

I never understood
how a vast collection of aromas
filling the air, consuming one room
manage to smell so divine
          blending to find
          one binding note
          that coats the store so evenly
          it'd be completely warm
               and worn all winter
dropping a different hint or two
every so often
figuring it would be smart to adapt
to different skin as people swatch it
swap it like the interchangeable
bands of their Apple wrist watches

while still managing to match the nuances
   of the original fragrance they sprayed
                  and make it last all day
the same way
your presence
        lessens
        distress
          quicker than the clicks heard
             when you enter a room
             covered in tile or wood

a sound that remains
ingrained in my imagination

like the sales pitch which
working women occasionally switch
while swapping those swatches of perfume
between hands
they watch as you rub your wrists together
discerning whether you'll remember
to come back for a full-sized bottle
or forget it once it dulls, dissipates
or disappears from the shelves

you are a household name

no wonder
it consistently sells out.

Did you know
a gift like yours--
if it were able to be duplicated
would be wrapped and sold at Saks
forever notable
stocked faster than a tourist could ask
for directions to Fifth Avenue
but it's innately you

sought by many who adore you...

I never understood
how a vast collection of aromas
filling the air, consuming one room
manage to smell so divine
in every designer store
with a perfume floor
or

how you delicately coat
a room with an endearing warmth

as if you immediately know
notes of snow
combine undeniably well
with the floral fragrance you bloom
year round

that must be how
you linger in everyone's mind
the scent wafting a meaningful memory
in their mind's eye

in my eyes

your presence
never fades

SUMMERS IN THE HAMPTONS

I go to the Hamptons
when I want to concentrate
on nothing but you.

That's what we all do…
when we want to get away from life,
right?

escape from the pressures of the actual world
just relax, enjoy the richness of quality time

adrift from society, daydreaming,
but somehow very much alive

vividly recounting details
of countless nights— days with you
as if you're walking right beside me

wandering inside BookHampton
for cover from the overcast weather
vigilant not to get your hair wet
based on the percentage of rain

hands glued together
stuck novel pages

thumbing through bookcases
hoping to find that quintessential
rainy day read
smile beaming

just to be there
exploring the East End
with you

then mentally steeping the tea
I know we'll drink— grabbing a cozy throw
to nestle up in when we arrive home

or going for a drive down Dune Road
to gush over the million-dollar mansions
style and decor

planning an evening at the LongHouse Reserve
Twilight Tour— unwinding in the dusk lighting
outdoors as gorgeous as you

what could be more luxuriously down to Earth
an adventure worth every word
I've ever written

following a picturesque night together
surrounded by wealth, greenery,
and nothing else.

no one
else.

Waking in the morning, to a note left in the foyer:

Meet me by the pool, honey.
xoxo

I swear I can hear your voice lifting
from your monogrammed stationary
as it travels to my ears

Without even trying,
you manage to tint my rosy cheeks
make me grin with all my teeth
until my face lovingly aches

I catch a glimpse of you through
the ornately framed bay windows
with thoughtfully chosen
porcelain
trim
and sheer curtains

you would most likely pick
for your home's interior

and I automatically know
that you embody
the most enchanting glint
of exquisite paradise

even your shadow cannot deny

in your negligee
adorned with lace.

and my goodness
I am the luckiest woman in the world

but only
when...

...i'm in the hamptons.

SINATRA POURS

In old New York the rain resembles
how I would imagine it feels

to kiss you
after the ball drops

confetti scattered through the air
people dancing everywhere

without a single care in the world
kissing, cameras panning to engagements
ringing in the new year with love—
in love

A Times Square bubble
wrapped between midnight and 12:01
exhilarated, popping Champagne
while the confetti settles
lining the gutters of each street

just as water drops draw
puddles on the sidewalk— nature's chalk

and Sinatra sings his annual ode
to another year in New York City

I would imagine
kissing you feels like

whistling to the
soundtrack of taxi
horns

or of children giggling
on the merry-go-round
    they stumbled upon

creating a fantasy world
inside their hotel's revolving door

        it feels
like an unspoken rule of New Yorker etiquette—
a mutual understanding that the locals have

when trekking under cover
as the raging downpour morphs
into a tempestuous storm

each person instinctively knows
to raise and lower their umbrella

      trying to prevent a collision
          on the *overcrowded*
        s l i p p e r y sidewalk

much like our silent agreement
to refrain from curbing my sentiments—
stomaching sediment

after a decade starved of
transparency finally quenched
when you said you'd still
                love me

                        no matter what
                          I had to say

my innermost thoughts reframed
          encased by the glass

I placed in your hands

when you never asked for the picture
but still held it anyway.

I imagine
kissing you feels
like a gentle feather floating
landing to your hand on my shoulder

as you reassure me
unequivocally

trusting the radiance of your face
lit up like the top of the Empire State
building intensity

as your earring
accidentally grazes my ear

I hear
a lullaby

created by
the you'll be fines

I know
I can believe —

pacifying the teething anxiety
gnawing at my psyche, sore gums

those you'll be fines mean
immediate ease

as tranquil as the sound of torrential rainfall
rapidly

sky scraping
the tallest of roofs
before soaking the pavement
below

keeping a steady beat
to the flow
the graceful tempo

of Sinatra
ringing in proof
the new year
has

gratefully begun

AN EVENING AT THE THEATER

I know

it's not my place to worry about you
like rushing through
a dinner reservation
to make it to
the Majestic Theater
before the lights dim
and the curtain goes up

disrupting the iconic overture, along
with the dirty looks you receive from other patrons
as if you left the bathroom
without washing your hands first.

while I walk to my seat
it's too dark to see
the usher motioning me to my proper place

regardless of the
obviously cheap flashlight
barely indicating my unreadable number
I make it through

rehearsing an acceptable way to love you
during intermission-- waiting
in the queue for the women's restroom
I wash my hands with soap

hoping I can respectfully return to my seat
lights flashing my genuine concern

indicating that
the second act of the show
is beginning shortly

I wonder
if you have someone

to be that deep cherry, Scarlet O'Hara pigmented
velvet curtain

a soft, consoling design which
ensures a safe, self-exploratory space
entertaining the origins of your
multi-faceted character

or even a person to be the dimmer switch
which operates the house lights on your command
allowing your complexion to rest

showcase your complexity
with an authenticity
that will leave audiences in awe of you

though when nobody else is around
to examine the playbill of your Broadway production

who reels you back in after the performance
who goes behind the scenes
who sits with you in the balcony

when the costume
and the make up

are seconds away
from being removed

who is your Nicky Arnstein
        leaving you yellow roses
        in the seclusion of your dressing room

when you finally need to bow

                do you
                ever bow?

                who handles the critics?

                                the
                                critic

                                the
                                heart-stopping
                                        harsh

            dead to the presses

                reviewer
                 in you—

 who has never once missed will call
 or a single dress rehearsal at all

  I wonder if you acknowledge
       the performance

                without the understudy
                     of judgment

                                self-sabotaging the lead

I worry you might be unaware
that the audience is emphatically cheering for you

that this flawless perfection
this continuously blockbusting, unstoppable show
is turning you into an overworked actor

it's feeding you
while silently eating you

a l i v e

MIRROR, MIRROR ON THE WALL

The mirror is a magical but dangerous place.

It allows your brain a glimpse
of what you look like from the outside,

but also

it allows you to spin a web
made by the spider of hyper focus
which disguises
every personally selected aspect of your appearance
the leering qualities only you can see

trapping you
in the faulty shelter of its satin.
when you stand in front of the mirror,
what does that pesky silk-spinning arachnid
gravitate towards?

Is there a running list of physical characteristics
it bedevils you into changing?

I can picture the gist of it.

Be Thinner
Look Younger
Be Prettier

And this scares me.

this presumption
believing you need
cosmetic enhancements
to delay what?

the advancement of age
an unhealthy fixation
on your least self-appreciated features

or generally any sign of a progressing life stage

the right to remain silent isn't beneficial
when you are the judge
and your own thoughts are the jury

it's not a crime to vocalize
your self-castigating internal dialogue

witch hunts for reasons to justify
your inability to recognize

your spell-bindingly
timeless beauty

we all have nit-picked the gnats of our appearance
made ourselves cringe a little bit when we see
something we classify
as undesirable

that's why being terrified of spiders
is a widely known and understandably

bone
curdling
fear

that is perfectly fine

What makes me
scratch my head at night
is the ever-growing batch of bites
the tiny fangs sinking under your skin
leaving bumps
of contrasting characteristics
which have consistently itched
and left a seemingly permanent scarring
swelling below the surface
long before and long since

I've been able to admit
how many years I've spent
unconvinced that I love you

more than I should

Although there is nothing wrong
with alteration in moderation,

it tremendously frightens me
and overwhelmingly alarms me
that

sometimes
I look at you

and see
a poisonous discoloration
an allergic reaction to those bites

which are expertly concealed
by your glistening skin

discreetly venomous

increasingly creeping
detrimental harm

to the woman, I have grown to admire

It is commonly acknowledged
among those who know you

that you are so
irrevocably dazzling,

it renders additional cosmetics
unapologetically redundant.

However, I do realize
that you don't share that opinion,
at least subconsciously

that you may never see what we all see
what I see —
when I look at you.

Over the course of multiple years, I have witnessed
(and heard)
the somewhat
absurd
ways

people claim

your appearance and personality
have changed

And this terrifies me.

Quite frankly,
it urges me
to abscond to your house

Break Every Mirror

and tirelessly trap each spider
that crawls from those shards
in a barricaded wrought iron cage

only to release them
when they vow to prey
exclusively on insects

instead of your head
then send them
far away from you

to replace
the newly unoccupied space
where a mirror firmly held the slightest
insecurity

securely in place

with my eyes.

I'm not a hundred percent certain
where the disconnect between you
and your reflection happens.

I'm not even clear about where it began.

but what I can understand

is that
these spiders weave
deceptively intriguing webs
pique their victim's interest
then pin them—
stuck
to intricate lies
instilling apprehension

by clearly appearing
at tension's
vanity

as tiny
seemingly unproblematic eggs
then
evolving
into pestering babies
that you start to notice
when you get
s l i g h t l y
too close

then
as fully grown
obnoxiously long–
leggéd adults

who inhabit your mind
who feed off your sight

to compensate
for their species' atrociously
terrible vision.

if you intently watch and listen to the genuine praise
those around you continuously resound

you will combat your
kidnapped vision

crack every egg
break every leg

and cherish yourself
the way you deserve to

the way the rest of us do.

I want nothing more in this world
than for you to be more straightforward
and kind to yourself.

the fangs, the fears,
the scars

that you see
are valid.

They are also tough patterns
which are just as difficult to weave
as they are to shatter.

please, just tell someone.
start with your own reflection
if you have to.

but i don’t
want to lose you

to a fucking plate of glass.

WHEN G-D MADE YOU

She probably took one look at you

gazed to the angels surrounding you
while she delivered you to the
secure sanctuary that your parents
formed with their arms

and proceeded to blast the Hava Nagila.

Raise your voice and sing!
Dance, everyone, dance!

Circling like an endless ride
inside a Disney teacup
with every angel who had a magical hand
in bringing you to Earth

joining together in jubilant celebration
of a rewarding day's work
doing the Horah.

That's what I would have imagined, anyway.

I mean, how else are you supposed to react
when you discover the formula
for earth-shattering beauty

with the precious reinforcements
of irresistible sweetness
and
a contagious sense
of tenderness,
an authoritative
serenity

all present within the same baby girl

You, my darling
have grown

to be
a special
kind of blessing.

You possess the unique ability
to walk into any room

and eliminate anything
remotely negative about it

by laughing
through

your equally contagious smile
which embellishes your face

when you are incredibly,
candidly carefree.

I wish
I could see it
more often.

Not only because seeing you elated
is beyond priceless to me
but because

it enhances your ability
to walk into any room
and spread your compassion
to everyone who occupies it

just by breathing.

I have not met one
single human being

who has been able to replicate
that affectionately infectious talent

it comes to you so naturally
it may as well function as oxygen
for everyone else you come across

surviving by the protection, supportability
which you, as the regulated guardian
balance within

everyone benefits
from the breath of your enthusiasm
your pure positivity to be engrossed in the moment

surrounded
by dear friends,
belovéd family

those you treasure

and those who have only
just made your acquaintance

but are perceptive enough to immediately recognize
how you magnetize

ears
hearts
eyes

as yours blink

offering the sincerest greetings
extending your well wishes

while interlocking fingers
colloquially squeezing
arms

doling out double smooches
I've missed yous
for each cheek

with the same boundless care

that your parents must've had
as they swaddled you—
introduced you to the world

When G-d made you she probably
summoned a minyan of angels
who joined in prayer, recited
the Shehecheyanu

marking the auspicious occasion
of your birth, gifting the planet
with your invaluable soul.

then watched proudly from above
while the family who was blessed
with the duty of welcoming

cradling rocking
you
beamed
as they received
the miracle they prayed for.

When G-d made you
she probably, quite deliberately
delivered you

with the purpose of fostering a bond
between each person you encounter
with an accepting, all-loving essence

the personification of—
and how
an Angel manifests

through your vivacious
and overflowing kindness

At least,
that's what I would have
imagined, anyway.

because it allows me to envision

G-d dancing with the angels
after creating the universal blessing
that is you.

PHOTOGRAPHS AND PHONE CALLS

Every so often, I will pick up the phone
to call you
and I tell myself
that I just want to check in
which is most definitely true…

However, I also find myself calling
because I want to have a fond

friendship which spans the
twelve-hundred-mile silence
that
s e p a r a t e s

us
I don't understand why but
the relationship we do have

has always

been like this

two ends of a telephone cord
snapping back when I walk too far
from the kitchen receiver— you hang up

mine remains off the hook

I look exceptionally silly
listening to your silence—
the dial tone

a lonely click.

if
I'm being perfectly honest,
seeing you in person
has become the most

stomaching dropping
adrenaline pumping

emotional rollercoaster

that I enthusiastically wait in line to ride
the loopty loops— the incline

the fear of fallout is worth it
every time

it is certainly bittersweet but
after I've been with you

I open priceless photo albums
and realize that my feelings intensify

that I must stand behind
and wait

to reach the top
in order to ride
again.

Otherwise
I'd be devastatingly miserable
for months—
months

that would become a painful signifier

of the fact that we are
far from close knitted.

we are the Royal Dansk cookie tin
a confection misleading
feeding the idea that snacks reside
hidden— in plain sight

deceptively inside
the laundry room cabinet

where we sneak to find
a slew of sewing needles

scraps of fabrics with patterns
that don't match

and a random assortment
of buttons in all sizes

except for the one
you're frantically searching for
when your most frequently worn top
pops a button smack dab in the middle
and you already have one foot
out the door.
I can never manage to erase
or just fully misplace
the Cannon
the seemingly unbreakable camera

carrying the decade old
image of loving you

So,
I work up the courage to pick up the phone
gathering inconspicuous scenarios

focal points

expertly positioned for the idyllic shot

the bullseye
which could have possibly prompted
an off-the-cuff call

as if buying all of Target
was what you meant to do on a quick trip

convincing yourself you needed each item in the cart
when really you only came to shop for the carton
of Häagen-Dazs coffee ice cream to devour
spoon shoveling into your mouth
without bothering to dig for a clean bowl at midnight
a recurring activity
which doesn't involve
admitting

how
all-encompassing-ly awful

It feels to miss you
from the pit of my stomach.
I finally gather the guts
to pick up the phone
with those crafted conversations
at my disposal
like the unnecessary amount
of grocery bags under my sink
waiting to be used for garbage

mentally called on at a moment's notice

so you don't have a reason to be off the phone
as quickly

or in case a spillage of word vomit
intercepts the line following your
"hi, honey"

It might seem foolish—

I should be more forthcoming
about wanting to know you
but
i become
high-strung
approaching
our friendship in actuality.

I'm afraid that you won't want to explore
who I really am
or that you'll talk about yourself
without earnestly expanding
elaborating
on your day to day
as if the line only carries communication
one way
or worse

that you'll find yourself listening
to my erratic rambling, but only be talking to me
because you somehow feel obligated
to do so.

I'm not entirely sure why
these feelings come up for me.

You're not the only one this happens with either.

although
you are the only person
who could realistically crumble me

if you stopped
picking up the phone…

when my thoughts drift
I look at photographs of you to

fill

the

void

your

p r o l o n g e d
absence

leaves in the unprinted Yellow Pages
of my subconscious

becoming a credit line for unafforded time
numbers tucked between meaningless statements
getting charged, overdrafted
by an unfilled gas pump

maintaining an infinite balance
robbing fuel

leaving me empty.

During time apart I recreate the
positive feelings you generate

resembling the sprints of laughter
you hear when kids race to pop bubbles
that emerge
from soapy wands

I imagine when you were still a brunette
it makes me grin—
sheepishly giggle that way
because you have always been blonde
to me
With each passing photograph,
I combine aspects of you into a still life
that captures city photography
to the caliber that Vivian Maier would.

Pictures that elicit patron reactions
which can only be compared to an elated schoolgirl
who has no homework assigned on a Friday

although
I learn the lesson
that the work free weekend
that giddiness

is temporary
Monday blues—
not seeing you

from outside the frame

are
difficult
to

pass

I retake the test
snap
until it saddens me enough
or I care about myself enough
to stop

I come to terms with the grade I have
though it was never the grade
I should have earned
or deserved

the cursive that preserves these marks
on my report card
they eventually turn faint

the A in dissipating your smile from my brain
the C in the sparkle in your eyes from my vision

the F in forgetting
the enthralling vanilla scent
of your former perfume.

I am held back
in Pre-K
finding another restaurant

we
dine
together

I revel in your presence
appreciate the present
of you with you

then miss you

so
I pull out those photographs
debate making a phone call
        in a concerted effort to
                        begin again.

TWENTY QUESTIONS

When speculating what it would be like to
genuinely get to know who you are...

I visualize both of us sitting on your couch
with a glass of wine, while a Billy Joel record
spins on the turntable,
and playing a game
of twenty questions.

I would commence the festivities
by weeding out the basics:

What is your favorite color?

I envision it being a shade of pink
It complements your skin tone
when you pair a blouse
of that shade with
white jeans.

Then, I would venture into the everyday essentials:
The junk food you can't live without
or your go-to coffee brand.

These are harder for me to guess
because you are notorious for not eating crappy foods
but there must be something…
everyone has something…

As far as the coffee goes, I assume that you'd
prefer Starbucks; the barista in me has a hunch
that you'd rather have a specialty drink.

Although you say caffeine has reliably
s t r e a m l i n e d   your *anxiety*

so
you most likely don't drink coffee
at all...

The next topic on my list would be learning
what culturally Jewish staples you keep stocked
in your kitchen.

Are you as crazy about a bagel
with lox and schmear as I am?

Rather emphatically,
I'm sure we could both agree,
Manischewitz pales in comparison
to any wine label in existence

In my next line of tipsy inquisition,
I would investigate your music taste—
swiping your phone

checking the repeatedly played tunes in your library
and rummaging through the other record boxes...

After I've perused your collection,
I'd inquire about your favorite pair of shoes,
and why you picked them.

The first that come to mind for me
are the stellar eggshell stilettos
with the gemstone almost oatmeal
beaded buckle

you paired with that pearly waist
clenching dress

I've never forgotten...

For the longest time, I've tried to deduce
how your ankles have survived in those
or any shoe you own

without breaking

Ever.

Oh, and while I'm at it, I'm thoroughly intrigued by
the timing of when you decided to go blonde?
was it a gradual process?

Is this how you managed to perfect
your seemingly effortless hair routine?
did you just emerge from a salon
with your signature platinum hue?

when did you incorporate the lustful lowlights, adding
such a body, delicate dimensions to your color code?

Now that we are both properly inebriated,
and I've spent an overdue portion of the night
gushing over your hair secrets...

what film or book
significantly changed your life,
and why?

What
is your greatest regret
in life?

I would never aim to upset you in any way,

but it is a strong belief of mine
that you can learn a considerable amount
about a person

based on their answer
to this understandably difficult question.

On the flip side, what is the happiest moment
in your life thus far?

I've even considered
what your college major was
and why you chose it?

I giggled unsure of its accuracy when we discussed this
Religious Studies just doesn't seem like it fits.

Selfishly,
I would like to uncover three main things
to playfully tease you about:

your guilty pleasure
your turn ons
your biggest pet peeve.

I would find myself apologizing preemptively
for my teasing while continuing to make them
anyway.

What is your favorite spot in New York City?

I imagine it would be somewhere that showcases design
you've indefinitely possessed a green thumb for flair.

If you could go anywhere else in the world,
but you had to leave instantaneously
Where would you go?

I picture you on a tropical island somewhere
Maybe Paris or Italy instead.
Although, I don't really know why.
I just do.

And lastly, I desperately want to know

How glorious you must look
when you wake up in the morning,

and

The last thing you do before bed after
a nightcap much like the one I imagine
when you're drinking wine on the sofa

with me.

SOMETIMES

when I am reunited with you
after being

s
e
p
a
r
a
t
e
d

for a while

the first thought
that pops into my head

is…

shit,

what I would do
for one chance
to make love to you.

I'm sorry if that's wrong for me to say…
it is—
I know it is—
wrong for me to say

but I want to be the one who kisses
the most intimate parts of you.

I want to ensure
that you feel appreciated
that you feel cherished
that you feel incomparably pleasured…

I wish to slide
my dominant hand
smoothly

just above my knuckles

from the center of your ear to the peak of your chin
following the delicate chisel of your jawline
then turn your head towards mine

as you lay, leaning— clasped
a jewel on the chain of a necklace
in my lap between my crossed ankles

x's to your o's
supported by the board of my chest
play me
like an intense game of tic-tac-toe
full of jest
hilarity
belly laughs
that gradually morph
into competitive shouting
until I concede

until I repeatedly
secretly

let you win

I will always let you win.

I wish to kiss you with all the magic
of an eyelash blow

both 11:11's
365 and 66

when an eventual leap year in February hits

with every airplane
I've mistaken for a shooting star

or a small meteor which
totally still works, by the way,
if the intention is purely placed

nonetheless,
I'd also wish on every actual shooting star
while they fleetingly journey
across an infinity of otherwise
blackened sky…

and with each changing phase
leading to the impending full moon
or even
the crescent
representative
of
the curve
in the small of your back

The lunar eclipse I wish to caress
while fishing like DreamWorks
puddles bubble floating
each individual vertebra

as sensitive
as an etch a sketch
that I'd shake again
and again

and again

frustrated but excitedly determined
to keep working with my creation
until it came out pristine

Then I'd sit
examine it
close my eyes
and animate
the diamonds in the sky
each feature of your skin
your complexion
a specific hue

not just blue
not just yellow
not just green

rather,
the way Vincent viewed them
filled with constellations
Van Gogh-ing with his third eye

making you
the swirling Aquarian
of a galaxy

far far away from me

Naturally, I did study
to become an astronaut— caught
in the black hole of meaningless equations…
since when did math
launch rockets with the engine of the alphabet?

what combination of letters
form the appropriate phrase

creating an orbit, a force
a drowsy current, or

a literary tidal wave— that submerges you into the dream

running a fever
the temperature of my desire
climbing higher than a
Mercury retrograde fire

until it reaches a planet
that hasn't been discovered yet

what tools
what language
would it take for you to find it
align your lips to mine
flip me
accidentally drape loose hair into my mouth
while topping—
position
your knee for stability

screaming
that penetrates the stratosphere
relinquishing my center of gravity

I do attempt to stave off the craving
the fruitful hunger that pangs for you

Though I am named after Eve
My Hebrew roots run so long
so thick so strong

Silverstein
would have to write a sequel
to the Giving Tree

keeping up with my growing linguistics
translating my prolific admiration

through divvying my apples
through offering my leaves
to the Queen
of this eternal forest

formed by my vocabulary
giving her everything
yet foraging
on
through branches intertwined
with high rises in the city
the seedlings of my every emotion
wood
building a penthouse
arks of pent-up adoration
until my paneling has no choice
but to crown
attending the coronation
for a house of royals

a multimillion-dollar view
you.

big apples never do
fall
far
from the tree.

the tiny hairs on the back of my neck
instinctively stand when our eyes meet

a fantasy of hands clutching bed sheets
arched spines
curled toes
heads thrown
back in ecstasy

cloud our reality from behind my lids
I feel your hair covering my bare skin
draped curtain bangs tied back, tucked
the sensation leading me to the edge

the resonance of your voice
has me hearing colors, possible paintings
whispering in my ear…

choking on my drink,
I return to the present moment
as we are seated at the table for our meal

I slowly sip my wine
while unsuccessfully trying
to regain control of my wild imagination.

It's unfortunate but I have come to learn
that i can only let it wander

sometimes

BOROUGHS OF ROMANTIC COMEDIES

the first time i truly *saw* you

my eyes immediately started
to play tricks on me.

from my sight line you resembled a cliché

a stereotypical scene
plucked out of a Rom Com
based in New York City.
You know,
the ones where everybody on the city street
is traveling in the opposite direction
of the principal character

and everything else other than
you
is
blurry
and playing
in

s l o w
motion?

My heart was transfixed
a nozzle attached
to a handheld vacuum

My lungs
became a sealed Ziploc bag
being drained of all its air.

It was almost as if

I
were finally
wide
awake
I'm not sure
how I was capable
of mindlessly sleeping before
maybe
it was the fact
that I unknowingly needed new glasses
correcting the outdated prescription

that must have been why
I couldn't see…
but how could that be?

when the billboard on my forehead gleamed

my cheeks and teeth betrayed me
divulging my deepest sentiments
revealing my widest smile

you'd have to be entirely oblivious
or legally blind
not to see
or how
each time
you call me *honey*
or *sweet girl*

i feel the reliably consistent flittering
the overpowering jittery joy

as if I coincidentally bumped into you

at *The Shop Around the Corner*
while trying to find shelter

from the serendipitous snowstorm
pausing my walk back home…

talking on the phone
slightly kills me
because every time we end a conversation
I feel like the girl who awkwardly tries
to act natural
and makes it painfully

worse

while grasping for any words
that could form a proper

goodbye

albeit slightly stuttering
hoping to generate the "right" sentence
from anywhere other than my actual head
but instead
replying with something akin
to
"I carried a watermelon"
so I force myself to breathe
before I commit to saying

love ya!
instead of

I
Love
You

making a conscious effort
to prevent myself
from seeming like a legitimate idiot

even though I already consider myself one
for knowing I love you in ways I shouldn't
but not being able to keep it under wraps
I stare
squinting
at an eye chart
hoping the blurred lines
come to focus on a table
where I sit with you

wary of your glasses

that
although, slipping down your nose
are still completely capable
of clearly appetizing
my innermost thoughts and fantasies
by magnifying
my view of your almond eyes
I instantly crack
as I watch you
peer over the frames
from across that high-def table
but definitely pretend
to be undecidedly glancing
at the menu
of the quirky little diner
we happened to stumble into

I'm not sure I'll ever be ready to order
I can't just "have what she's having"
enjoy the show from the back of the theater

with all the tall people blocking the screen
regardless of the stadium seating

I can clairvoyantly see
my heart seeping
the ink of my adoration

a hopeless romantic's thinning blood
infected by storyline retention
while the plot thickens

bouncing off the projector
skimming the blue light film of your glasses
skipping rocks, the dilated pupils of
my
hazel
eyes
inexplicably boomerang
tears straight out of The Notebook
smacked

with an anemia hijacking red cells
emotions that felt so shockingly close
to how I saw my fictional future

growing older with you

I managed to stay conscious
to remain inside the movie
where I'm still protected
by the film trope of you

walking beside the hazy city dwellers
unable to tell who is headed in
the opposite direction
never paying attention

from across the busy avenue
as the opening credits signal lights
policing the crosswalk
which makes reaching you virtually impossible

we already know it's far more practical to gamble
playing Russian Roulette with traffic
unwaveringly weaving

through
the
uneven
lanes

carelessly speeding in a blind effort
to successfully find you

mirroring the principal character
courting their romantic interest

scripted

in the lights
camera
action

of a popular Rom Com based in New York City

THE TIMES DEFINES LOVE

I loved you
before I ever

Loved
you

and through loving you

I learned what it felt like
to be the Sunday *Times*

every time
that paper smacked my doorstep
it would hit me
as quickly

as Barnes & Noble's book smell

No matter where or when I came across it
I continued to be reminded of the untouchable bubble
which has always been my happy place growing up
as a grown up

who knew my main production of serotonin
would come from my local Barnes & Noble
The New York Times
and
the wonderfully irresistible
yet dependably mysterious
world of your mind

where the extent of your fondness never dies

my love
skimmed through arts and leisure
until it aimlessly meandered
into Starbucks at the bookstore

and found significantly more
than what it bargained for
it sought
after a compassionate history
searching within the foam
of the delicious vanilla cappuccino
she ordered
instead
she left the café with a mystery so perplexing

even Sherlock was rummaging through
the coffee-stained pages empty cups relaying
this case may be unsolvable
since the lines

I loved you
before I ever

Loved
you

perpetually remain smudged

I can only attempt to explain how I love you
by comparing you to the scaffolding
holding my soul in place
as I continue to expand
upon it

the construction crew
planned out this build
meticulously

yet, structurally

issues repeatedly
seem to creep around each
corner

leaving the only thing they're certain of
being that you are the solid foundation

you can imagine the frustration
as they try to figure out why
we're still shaking
aching
to explore every floor
but unsure
of the support

due to so many changes in the prints
as our building ages
and no progression
toward ending stages
are rendering results that last

they are completely aware your care wouldn't dare falter

the blueprints
indicate
a budgetary restriction
quickly amassed

prompting the stopping of all construction

the only thing building
is a passionate stagnation

due to the admiration of your marvelous soul

I loved you
before I ever

Loved
you

and now that I love you…
while also

Loving
you

folding sections
of the New York Times
while I sip my ritualistic vanilla cappuccino
reminds me of the story printed between the pages

the sacred margins
of your comforting embrace

the state based
where the most reputable newspaper
circulates

today's **boldface**

covers
love

TO THE WOMAN FROM LONG ISLAND

To the woman from Long Island
who makes *how are yous*
sound like Gin Beach waves

whose lips
taste the tongue tides
in my For Five Manhasset
iced coffee

with a vocal timbre
as dreamy as the Sunken Meadows boardwalk
silhouettes of Connecticut— lush evergreens
sounds of dawn infinitely serene

a horizon personified
the ferry goers can only hope to catch
soak in— on their way back to Manhattan
a repose which goes without saying

To the woman from Long Island
whose presence moves the moon

a luminous spirit, a riveting belle
fire bright like the South Bay lighthouse
guiding ships at sea

describing what it means to dive headfirst
into the moment, go for unintentionally long
aimless drives, alone yet together
expressed in her best way
laughing
w i t h n o n a v i g a t i o n
but the rest is yet to come

To the woman from Long Island
who symbolizes serenity's birth
remember your refreshed golden roots

surrounding towns with fervor
   fertile, flourishing lily beds
   Westbury seedlings
            receive

   blossoming an enchanted
      whimsical bouquet

turn
to the woman from Long Island
                they said
she
will flower peace
unlike any you've ever known

CENTRAL PARK

Every time we touch
my pulse quickens
circulating memories
conveyed
by your beguiling
eyes

a chestnut metropolis
which has me falling
smitten
with
the coziness
of their belovéd
autumn

The affluent endearment you emit
reminds me of sitting in Central Park

auburn and glints of orange
new England brick
cool weather, brisk

hot latte burned lips
accentuate those rich,
coffee-colored eyes

I lose myself
fantasizing in

when my heart begins
to miss
the city

as heavily as it misses you

The billowing breeze of the park trees
flows through your cascading curls,

and I am met
with an overwhelming sense
of delight.

The natural ambiance
represents an exquisite nature
much like the one
you seem
to believe
that everything
needs to be idealized
f l a w l e s s l y
seen from the outside

even when
you pretend to be perfectly fine,
d i v i n e
while burning internally

It's almost as if your mind is the clique of little kids
climbing on the rocks during peak summer season

palms ignited
red, but determined to reach the pinnacle
losing their grip—
fragile balance
which leads to scraping their knees

bleeding
realizing they should have listened to their parents
who suggested they run along the path

play a game tag instead

heading down those ominous tunnels
when the park is dark
only reinforces

the echo of horses galloping
sounding like you're being followed
by the carriage of nerves and sorrow

although tomorrow

you'll attract
the inspiration for the autumn air
feel
the blades—hair
lying flat
in the grass
enveloped by the ravishing romance
shared between flowers & fairytales

couples who leisurely spend their day
cuddled up to clichés on the benches
alluring their senses to the scents of the season

the reasons
I have loved you

these precious memories of when I
laid my eyes on New York City initially

Nothing has been able to replicate that
visceral inner knowing, I'm home

until you...

WHEN A POET LOVES YOU

When a poet loves you
their mind itches to immortalize you on paper.

Their hands burn with the desire to write
every word that can't be spoken.

It stems from a deeply personal, cathartic place
and drastically lessens the overwhelming urge we feel,
to suppress or drown our powerful emotions.

It also allows us to illustrate
our profound amorousness toward you
in a meaningful and eloquent way.

I might be a bit biased, but I have found,
that the best way to emphasize the extraordinary
impact you've made on someone is to get a poet
to write about you.

***

I am tremendously proud to call you the woman I love.

However unrequited, I'd confidently profess
how my feelings for you came to be
if making such an outright confession

aside from creative expression, wouldn't drastically
change the incomprehensible value of the relationship
I do have with you and those who

surround you

so,

i'll keep writing

to you

as if

there is more between us

than the sincere words

printed

on these

pages

It soothes me greatly to know
that if no one ever publishes this,
the people who do read it

will be able to experience your exhilarating aura
even if they never have the privilege of meeting you
in person.
or maybe
even be blessed
with the cherished honor
of loving you as I do

I quite enjoy the idea
the possibility– that the people who do know you
will read this too and not realize
it was written about you.

However,
My greatest ambition
as it relates to preserving you on the page
is not only that you continue to live on

after we are both gone

but more so
that you find an immeasurable sense of contentment
at a pivotal point in your life.

for you to care for, adore yourself

u n c o n d i t i o n a l l y

If that means telling you how I feel one day,
and possibly sacrificing any chance of having
a meaningful friendship with you—I would do
it without hesitation.

I wholeheartedly hope that one day
I will have the chutzpah to give you this book.

I pray that
although you will never
share the sentiments for me
that I do for you

my poems
will help you recognize

how e x c e p t i o n a l l y loved
beautiful you are...

from behind
your city eyes

www.21chieftanspress.com
@21chieftanspress

Acknowledgments

I consider myself incredulously lucky to know the woman this collection is about. Without her, my life would never be the same. This is my best way of thanking her.

Mom, thank you for being my cheerleader and for modeling how to achieve your dreams. You were my first loyal reader and have read everything I've ever written. I love you more than all those words put together.

To my *Daddy* and my *Grandma,* the avid reader you fostered since I was a little girl has finally become the writer you believed in. I miss you both, and you are forever in my heart.

Jake, you have been a pillar throughout my life as well as my book journey. I couldn't have asked for a more caring brother, let alone a twin, who has been by my side through every milestone.

To my *Aunt Gitta* and *Uncle Danny*, there aren't enough words to explain how lucky I am to be loved by both of you. Being your niece has not only given me an unbreakable family bond with you, Nicole, and Tony, but also it gave me an invaluable support system while writing this book and beyond.

Aunt Meryl, thank you for reading this book with an honest take and encouraging me to pursue my aspirations. You were the lightning force who struck me out of the dark and were always there to steer me onto the right path, even when I didn't want to choose it. I appreciate that more than you know.

Aunt Carol, you protected my heart when writing these poems inflicted such deep emotional injury, that I wanted to shatter every ounce of its sensitivity. Thank you for communicating the value in fiercely caring for others and for dependably holding me together.

To *Alex, Christina,* and *Marty,* having your family in my life is such a wonderful present. In addition to caring for my brother's happiness, you cared for mine, and it helped make my dreams a reality.

Marlene, you have been the tallest sunflower in a field of challenging seeds. Thank you for guiding me as I grow, and for keeping my Grandma's memory alive.

Grandma Lana, the unwavering love and support you have shown me and my writing, is by far the most precious gift I have ever received. Thank you for embracing me as your additional Granddaughter. Having a Grandma again, let alone one who is as amazing as you, is such a blessing.

Risa, you were a beyond special person and the most wonderful Bonus Mom. I am immensely grateful to have had you in my life. I will forever strive to make you proud.

Tori, thank you for being the best preliminary editor and confidant that a writer could ever ask for. You are an irreplaceable friend. I absolutely adore you.

Hollis, thank you for my stunning cover and for giving me the courage to ensure that my book and I got resources we deserve. You are an exceptional human being.

To the *one who loves her*, thank you for your accepting mind and heart. Even if you decide to not read this version of the book, I am grateful for your willingness to read the earlier draft, and for always being someone I can count on.

About the Author

Sarah Erin is an LGBTQ+ love and mental health poet who resides in New York City. She draws upon her hopeless romantic nature in conjunction with her provocative side to capture the multifaceted landscape of her relationships (with herself) and with other women.

Sarah takes pride in her writing as well as her three adorable fur babies: Philip, Tony, and Evelyn. Her drive to explore the intricacies of the English language has inspired her most cherished hobbies, propelled her aspirations, and prompted her journey of self-discovery.

She is also the author of the viral semi-autobiographical TikTok novel ***Beyond the Table***.

<u>Social Media:</u>

TikTok: @saraherin.poet
Instagram: @saraherin_thepoet
Wattpad: @sarahepoet

www.saraherinauthor.com

www.ingramcontent.com/pod-product-compliance
Ingram Content Group UK Ltd.
Pitfield, Milton Keynes, MK11 3LW, UK
UKHW041851190726
13854UKWH00002B/841

9 798218 170615